The Subjective Truth of the Esoteric Self

a meditative guide to wellbeing

by john baltisberger

A Kaiju Poet Publication

This book was written and self published by John Baltisberger

Copyright © 2020 John Baltisberger
Edited by Lisa Lee Tone
Foreword by Lucas Mangum
Cover Art by Roomyana

All rights reserved. No part of his book may be reproduced or used in any manner without written permission of the copyright owner except for the use of quotations in a book review. For more information, address: john@madnessheart.press

First Edition
www.kaijupoet.com

John Baltisberger

This book is dedicated to Naturre G. whose peace came at too high of a price. May your memory be for a blessing and may you forever ride horses across the eternal plain

Foreword

I refer to my stories as Coping Mechanisms for the Apocalypse. People find solace in horror, escape, catharsis. This is the use of fiction, and it's especially crucial during these scary times. However, simply indulging in entertainment is only a portion of the ritual for one who aims to truly better themselves, manage their emotions, and continue existence when the world is on fire and everything hurts.

Overindulging in escape can often lead to the opposite of the desired result. It doesn't work like it used to. You become numb to it, and the malaise comes creeping back in. That's because fiction can treat symptoms, raise questions, and help us understand the world a little better, but it doesn't treat the cause or have answers. Indeed, oftentimes fiction that provides answers is propaganda masquerading as such (looking at you Ayn Rand). Enter John Baltisberger. I met John at Killer Con 2019. I was coming off the release of my Splatterpunk-Award-nominated novella Saint Sadist. He was making his first convention appearance as a publisher.

He had a lot of interesting things to say, and I loved that he was there to make friends. While he did have a table, he seemed far more interested in meeting people and having conversations than simply selling books and moving on. That's because John cares about people. What you hold in your hand is essentially a self-help book. I avoid this genre like the plague.

It's full of would-be gurus and prosperity gospel frauds who just want your money. I'm sure there are good people as well, but you've got to wade through a lot of muck to find those unmuddied souls. Frankly, it can be a lot of work, especially if you don't know who's behind the message. Since Killer Con 2019, John has become a collaborator, friend, and publisher. We've had several conversations about the nature of reality, social responsibility, and the pitfalls of small-press publishing. There is a through-line in all our interactions. I see a guy who genuinely wants to better himself and help guide people who want the same.

I see a well-read guy who takes spirituality very seriously but won't beat you over the head with it. He is, without a doubt, one of the aforementioned unmuddied souls. With this book, he's collated everything he's learned on his ongoing spiritual journey in the hope that some of these things will help others. His intentions are noble; his advice, practical; and his prose is easy to digest. He's going places, and he wants to help others do the same. You may already know John from his works of splatterpunk and bizarro horror or his Jewish kaiju poetry.

Those works all do what fiction should do: they treat symptoms, raise questions, and help us understand the world a little better; but for those who wish to go further, he has something for you too. You'll find it here in The Subjective Truth of the Esoteric Self.

-Lucas Mangum, 10/22/2020, Texas

Introduction

This book is not meant to be read from beginning to end, not really. While the lives we lead in the physical world are seen as following a linear timeline, the truth of our spiritual and mental selves is somewhat different. Though we wake up, live our day, and go back to bed according to the same clock that we collectively as a cluster of societies have agreed to follow, our conscious selves rarely, if ever, adhere to this schedule. We spend our days daydreaming, casting ourselves into the uncertain future; we dream of mistakes that have not happened or fantasize about miracles that may never come. Or we dwell on the past, taking ourselves out of the already decaying moment to revisit things we have no power to change. We are, as Vonnegut put it, unstuck in time.

Similarly, this book follows no concrete flow. It has been divided into sections, and each section into segments.

    The first section, Concepts, is intended to introduce key concepts in meditative and esoteric thought that will be useful to you. While we start abstractly with our perception of time, we move swiftly to the self, and then to the whole of the universe and reality itself. It is written in an order that I feel would be useful in working oneself up from that which is apparent to that which is discovered. Each segment a part of the whole picture. While each segment of this section has had entire libraries of philosophy, theology, and thought written, these are meant to be concise, to start your journey or to provide sustenance for your mind while you meditate.

    The second section, Rituals, introduces various forms of meditative practice. While we have the mental image of the Buddhist monk sitting lotus style before a statue of the Buddha, hands in esoteric positions as incense rises all around, this is far away not the only way to meditate; indeed, it is not even an easy way to meditate for most. Not every manner of meditation is right for every person, and one may find oneself drawn to one more than others. Conversely, perhaps, you will find that you need to do combinations or alternating forms of meditation in order to stay interested or to find time for a practice. The important thing is the doing, not the manner in which it is done.

With the key concepts in mind and a manner of practice we find useful to us, we can embark on the practical use of meditation. The third section, Obstacles, focuses on those things that interrupt the flow of our peace. Those moss-covered stepping stones that seek to trip us on our path to unity with the greater whole of reality. This is by no means an exhaustive list, but most issues may find their root in these emotional blockades. The entire goal of this book is for you to be able to step away from these emotional speed bumps and come to a place where you can overcome them with the least harm to the physical, mental, and spiritual self.

Each segment contains some information on the topic and how we can view it within our own subjective truth, followed by a guided meditation on that topic. In this way, you may move through the concepts and obstacles that interest or speak to you, taking the fruit from the forbidden tree which offers you the knowledge you seek for yourself. It is my hope that this will allow you to find the words you need, when you need them, without having to hunt for hours. This book was made as small as possible so that it could fit in a pocket or purse, so that it could be available when and where you needed it. No matter where you are reading—on the bus, at a restaurant, or sitting on a cushion in your own home—you should feel comfortable opening this book, taking what you need, and then abandoning it until you feel you need more.

Though my own path to hidden truth lies through Judaism, you will find little, if any, overtly religious tones in this book, nor will you see strictly Buddhist teachings. Rather, the teachings, meditations, and truths within this book follow a winding path through many faiths and beliefs; secular, religious, and self-discovered. While I have spent years exploring philosophy, theology, and metaphysics, you do not need to, not in order to find peace, not in order to meditate, and certainly not to be happy. It is much easier to contemplate these concepts and topics when we turn our minds to them, it is much harder to keep the peace of oneness with nonexistence in sight while actively living and in the moment. Perhaps this book will help center you when you need the assistance.

Remember that in all things, the most important goal of this book is your well being, and the most important truth of the esoteric self is that it is subjective.

Take a moment to examine this book. Allow your preconceptions of meditation, spirituality, and esoteric thought to fall away. Feel the book in your fingers; what does it feel like? Is it new or worn? Is this the first time you are reading these words or the hundredth? Consider the reason you are reading it. Understand that your motive colors your understanding of the content. Close your eyes and simply feel pages of the book between your fingers. Each page is covered in words and those words have meanings beyond that assigned to them through conventional language.

Become aware of your breathing, and of the feeling of the floor or chair beneath you. These sensations have always been there, waiting for you to notice them. Similarly, your true self and your peace are in existence currently, simply waiting to be noticed and acknowledged.

Open your eyes once more, examine your needs in this precise moment. Flip to the section you feel would help you the most. Discover the truth as it exists for you.

John Baltisberger

Concepts

Past

There is arguably nothing in this reality more subjective than the past, other than, perhaps, the truth. They say those who do not remember the past are doomed to repeat it; however, I argue that there are few powers that can stop people from repeating their past, both on a personal level and a global one. Perhaps we believe we can do things different the next time, perhaps we feel our past mistakes were flukes. Whatever the case may be, we must understand at an intrinsic level that we are wrong. The past does not exist, it is an abstract idea, assimilation of the memories you have chosen to retain. The past's only worth in reflection or study is to understand how the current circumstances have come to exist and offer options for addressing those circumstances.

But its worth is not what makes the past subjective. Rather, it is the processing of information through several lenses. The first lens is that of memory itself. Few people have perfect memories; the information of the past is taken, and information that is important to the individual is saved or given greater importance than data that is less pertinent. Then that which is saved must go through the emotional and opinionated psyche of the human mind. This nuanced reality that is created, a story that has already happened and gone, is unique to each individual and worthless where the truth is concerned.

However, there is a deeper truth: as the past exists only in our memory, which is a current construction of our conscious mind, the past is constantly existent in the present. There is no past, there is only the present story of how this moment came to be. If you consider time in terms of a book which you read, you can begin to understand. We speak of 'earlier in the book,' but the truth is that all of the book—past, future, present—

is currently within the pages. There is no true time to a book, only the time that we assign to it through our interpretation of the symbols and conventions of literature that we have grown to accept.

You are not the past; the past is simply a story told within your consciousness to explain the reality you are currently experiencing around you. When you consider the self, you must consider only that exact moment, as anything else is either dead or potential not yet realized. Even the moment you have read this word, the words that came before them exist in your memory. They are still there, happening in the same space and time, but they are now in the past.

Even still, the past can be a useful concept in your meditation, or perhaps a cause for meditation. One may experience a feeling of despair due to an event they perceive as being in the past. Or perhaps a moment of tranquility could be an anchor to a peace that one could use to find those moments of truth and strength. But we must always be diligent to remember that the past's importance is only in understanding the present. No more. No less.

Take a moment to clear your mind of any hopes or daydreaming about what may be. Before we delve into the past, we must abandon the future. Recall a memory, this could be a good memory or a bad memory, but one that is vivid in your mind. Attempt to consider this memory without emotional weight. When you feel yourself growing invested in the memory, step back from it. Recognize that this memory is not happening now, that it is not your present reality, and reconsider it dispassionately. Seek to find details that had hidden themselves from your emotion laden recall. Find the color of the sky, or the facial expressions you had not considered important before. Through the unemotional scrutiny of your memory, seek to uncover new aspects of your reality, new joys in your happiness, and new understanding in those things. Freeze the memory in place and move about it, realize that while you could not have seen these angles and moments before, they are clear now, you can control how the memory plays out. With this realization comes understanding that the memory is a creation not of the objective truth that has happened but rather the subjective perception of something that has happened.

As you take your time exploring this construction of a memory, take away aspects that are no longer important once emotional investment is gone. What stands out to you? What colors are prevalent? Can you feel the memory, taste it? Allow even those important aspects of the memory to slip away. What is left? What constructs from your mind are left as you strip away the things that matter to you from the memory? You are left, and yet you are not your memory, you are not the past. You have taken yourself from that memory and remain whole.

John Baltisberger

When you are ready, return to the present and continue the current truth.

Present

If the past is nothing but a story that exists purely in the memory of the present, then surely the present must exist. This, too, is an illusion based solely on a need to quantify existence by the strictures of time as we have been taught throughout our lives. Mindful meditation teaches us to become aware of things as they exist in the moment. To take in sensations. Consider, however, that a sensation is an external stimulus; it touches us, and then an electrical signal pulses and travels to our brains. By the time we are aware of the sensation, the initial "present" of what caused it is gone to the annals of the past.

In this way, every sensation and stimulus we have is simply a memory of something that happened. It may not be possible to even grasp the present; instead, we react to things in the immediate past or impulsively anticipate the immediate future. This is as close to 'living in the present' as we can be through our existence as temporal beings. Even the thoughts we have exist only in our memory, for the moment they have passed, they are gone. What do we do with this information, how do we reconcile our inability to experience the present?

While troubling in terms of experiential existence, it is vital to remember that the weight of our reality does not rely on our experience. Does a stone experience the world as we understand it? No, yet it exists. Likewise, there is no need to slip into existential dread over the nature our own experiences. Rather, come to peace with it and through that peace seek a truth that speaks to you. Secure in the knowledge that your experiences are in the past, you may begin the work of bringing your existence more in tune with the immediate.

At any moment, you may ask yourself, "Am I dwelling on a sensation from the immediate past that has no urgency?" or "Am I anticipating something in the immediate future that has not occurred?" Again, as temporal beings whose awareness exists in linear time, we must be aware that some sensations and anticipations require urgency. A hand on an open flame, a car approaching us, these sensations and events, while not actually in the present, require that we react. But do we need to react to all things with the same urgency? Do we need to live in anticipation, pre-reacting to a conversation when the past sensation of the phone ringing reaches our minds?

By understanding the non-immediacy of all of our external and internal stimuli, we may distance ourselves from the past and future in thought. We can begin to divorce ourselves from the idea of who we have been and what we will be and instead focus on the ever-shifting moment we wish to be involved in at that very moment. Again, we must examine the self within the preconceptions of the present. The present is something we experienced in the future and anticipate in the past, it is an action that is already done, something we did, and therefore, we are not the present.

Find a place where you can sit or stand uninterrupted; turn off music, the TV, the phone.

Choose a single word that encapsulates your current desired state of mind. Take a deep breath and close your eyes, notice that you can feel your eyes moving under the eyelids. This sensation close to the brain is near immediate. Become aware of your autonomic functions. Your heart beats, you breathe. Take control of your breath and notice the sensation of breath entering your lungs, the expanse of your chest, the rise and fall of your shoulders with each full breath in and out. Feel the fabric of your clothes moving as you breathe; what does the texture against your skin evoke?

Notice the feeling of your skin against the floor, pull your awareness to the feeling of tightness in certain muscles and tendons. Where are you carrying pain? How does that pain present? After noticing and acknowledging each sensation, both pleasant and uncomfortable, pull your full awareness to your thoughts. When you feel your attention moving to a sensation, gently correct yourself to come back to a focus on your thoughts.

Like a pin, allow your thoughts to start broadly, then focus your consciousness to a point. Consider the word you have chosen; what are its connotations? What is its sound? Any distractions from the base theme of your word, allow them to drift away. Focus your intention and thoughts to a point, allow the word you have chosen to grow in size until it is all that fits in your present state of mind. There is nothing else but your word. You see it, you hear it, you are it. Allow your entire state to be subsumed by the word until there is no difference between the self and the sound. Then allow even that to fall away.

When you are ready, take your time to open your eyes, rediscovering the self and the world around you in that present moment.

Future

If both past and present are actually artifacts of memory and do not exist, surely then, the future is the only truth in existence. Constantly flowing out of potential and into the present, the future contains all possible scenarios we may experience. And yet, they have not happened. While any reality may exert itself in the next moment, it has not yet, and, therefore, does not exist in any meaningful way. We obsess over the future as much as we wring our hands over the past, dreaming of triumphs that can only exist within the confines of our dream world. In the future, we are the wittiest story teller, the most seductive person, and the greatest fighter to have ever lived.

Many people live their entire lives looking forever for this idealized figure they have built of themselves in the future. They believe that this figure will exist, it will become reality. But because they only dream of what they will accomplish, they never drag the action required out of the realm of thought and into the reality of action that could move them towards that figure. By idolizing themselves, they convince themselves they need no work to become better, because in the future, when the moment comes to prove, their idealized self will triumph.

Here we see that focusing on the future is not only flawed because the future does not exist in any meaningful way but also because it stymies the action that might make it meaningful by its very existence. Only by forsaking the anticipation of something that does not yet exist may we bring what we anticipate into the reality that we are experiencing. This is what is most commonly meant when someone instructs someone to live in the moment. It is advice to be happy for what you have, to be aware of the stimuli that is more immediate than the idea that some other stimuli may come eventually. With our eyes ever turned forward instead of inward, we end up missing the sensation that we anticipated before this moment within our past.

The future has worth only as goalposts that we must act currently to reach. By using the future to ensure we are working in the present, we engage in a constant act of self-betterment, whatever that goal of betterment may actually be. By understanding that the future is potential but requires the kinetic energy of our own movement towards that future, we may engage in healing the world and tending to our own wounds to attain the spiritually healthy self we long for. This idealized version of ourselves, who we wish we could be, exists in a completely subjective realm of non-existence. However it possesses the potential to exist, we move through our lives towards a reality that we either do or do not work for.

Thus, the future, by our own realization, is only a tool by which we can focus on the self. For by understanding what we wish we were, we can grapple with what we perceive to be our shortcomings. Those with no desire for change do not daydream of a possible future. We exist not only as potential but as a completed moment and an ongoing vibration that, in effect, stimulates reality as we are in turn stimulated. With this in mind, we must be aware that we are unable to identify ourselves as the future in any but the most allegorical sense.

Fix the idea of your future self in your mind's eye. Are they recognizable as you? What about them has changed from the you that is now? Do you believe this future you is more deserving of space and time than the present? Consider how this self is a reflection not of your desires but of your subjective view of your self-worth. Would others view this future self of yours in the same light? Consider the flaws that are present in your future self. Are they new due to changes brought by what you wish you had?

The Subjective Truth of the Esoteric Self

Or are they exaggerated weaknesses that you have amplified due to self-doubt?

By recognizing both your self-doubt and self-aggrandization, you are now able to remove them from the future you. This future self that is now in your mind's eye is more in line with your current potential. Honestly assess who this future self is. Is this worth the work it will take to realize it into the present? Is this new future self, free of the foibles of your ego, someone you still wish to become? Understand that this potential exists in the coiled springs of your psychic and spiritual self. See yourself unfurling like a net to enfold and capture this future self and bring it into you. Be aware of the worth that this self has and through that, realize that self-worth is already within you.

When ready, face the world with the potential of the future at your fingertips.

Breath

Coming to the awareness that time is a meaningless construct of our own consciousness, a useful tool for ordering our experiences and nothing else, we have also discovered through introspection that the past, present, and future are not included in the makeup of our being. We now turn from the abstract concepts of time to breathe. Breath is a key component of mythical story telling. In Abrahamic faiths, God pushes their breath into the nostrils of the first humans, granting them life. Breath is tied to life, voice, song. Every plant and animal breathes in some fashion. We assign so much importance to it as it connects us to so many different aspects of action.

Consider the breath first as a purely mechanical thing. Your lungs expand, sucking in oxygen and carbon dioxide and whatever else is near. The lungs deposit the oxygen into your blood, which is then pumped through your body by your heart. The oxygen feeds your organs and heals your wounds. You breathe out, your lungs contract, your diaphragm expands, carbon dioxide is expelled, and the process continues. This is your breath from a subjectively literal point of view. This process is autonomic, though we can take control of it, unlike our thoughts or our heartbeat. We may hold our breath, we may change the speed of our breath; it is, for all intent, our own to control.

But the breath connects to so much more; it connects us to each other. Through our breath, many of us are given voice; we can articulate our thoughts, communicate with others, and tell stories. Is it any wonder that the breath takes on mystical importance in our minds? Legends tell of witches that steal breath, and in Hebrew, the soul is called the "Ruach" or breath. We assign importance to our breath by the power we give it rather than in accordance to the function. Yes, we must breathe to continue living within this reality and continue our temporal journey; however, it is merely a function of that temporal existence. We communicate and tell stories without any need to expend our breath, why then do we continue to view breath as the means of life when the electrical impulses within our nervous system are more important?

Our breath is something that is easy to focus on, it is easy to hear, feel, it is an intangible thing that we experience none the less. Thus, the breath is a nearly perfect analog for our consciousness, or in some terminology, our souls. We may apply the workings of the body to the concepts of the breath. Reality expands, there are new consciousnesses within it, those consciousnesses spread throughout existence, either healing or harming as is their nature. Then reality contracts, and there are fewer consciousnesses, as lives or souls leave to the next understanding of the world. In this way, the universe breathes and we are each a part of the oxygen that flows through this reality. However, it is important to note that breathing is something we do, breath is something we possess, ergo, we are not the breath.

Bring your focus onto your breath, notice the natural rhythm, notice the feeling of your body expanding and contracting. Now, focus as you breathe. First allow your diaphragm to relax and expand as you inhale through your mouth. Only once the diaphragm has finished expanding, allow your chest to rise and expand as well. Your lungs fill completely. Hold the breath, count to five, and then breathe out of your nose. First allow the chest to deflate, and then contract the diaphragm to fully push out the air. Another five seconds. Each full breath in and out should take twenty seconds, allowing you three full breaths a minute.

Continue breathing and counting as

long as you need to find the rhythmic pattern of breath. Allow your entire focus to be on the bodily functions of breathing and then the counting after. There are no problems. There are no stresses or anxieties. There is only the breath.

Next, on the inhale, visualize the oxygen you breathe in flowing freely through your body to areas of tension. Feel the muscles unknotting as oxygen rich blood floods the area and heals the damage your temporal existence has done. Allow this visualization as you hold the breath. Every ounce of oxygen you take in goes to repairing damage and maintaining you. As you exhale, visualize your breath as a cloud of smoke, made up of the poisons you normally ingest. Doubt, anger, and resentment flow from you alongside carbon dioxide, loosened and then broken apart by your breath to now be expelled. Your next breath floods your brain, awakening creativity and invigorating your willpower. In this way, continue to breathe in healing and exhale pain. Focus on those parts of the body that cause you

chronic pain. Break apart the mental trauma that exists there.
As it is carried away, it dissipates like smoke on the wind.

When you feel fully refreshed, allow your breath to fall under autonomic control once more, and rejoin the physical world as it is for you.

Body

We exist in the physical world as bodies. We take up physical space, we have mass, density, and form. Our bodies exist in unity with our minds and spirit. If our body hurts, then we accumulate stress and find it difficult to concentrate and to relax. Likewise, if we feel stress, it can manifest as health issues, weight gain, or issues such as insomnia.

Often, we are taught to consider humans as specialized creatures, if someone is intelligent, they are weak. If someone is very strong, they are likely stupid. And the spiritual are usually one or the other. But this is a fallacy; a study[11] in the Frontiers in Human Neuroscience journal has shown the connection between cognition and fitness. When we ignore our physical body in order to devote ourselves fully to study or creative endeavors, we do so at the detriment of our

---
1   1

intellectual and spiritual self.

Likewise, when we focus solely on our physical bodies but do not feed our intellect, we become mono-tasked, failing to live up to the full potential of our current embodied incarnation. While insects are designed to specialize into specific tasks, the human body is instead a multi-tool, capable of tremendous mental, physical, and spiritual feats. But only when properly maintained will the body fortify the mind and soul, allowing for the unity of experience and interaction with the three worlds, or the material, cognitive, and ephemeral.

Consider what your body is. As multicellular incarnations of life and vibration, we are a constantly evolving, dying, and being reborn entity. Similarly, our ability to live and evolve is based on the workings of our body. Like a machine, when maintained, a body fires off electrical signals and carries out the wishes of the mind. But

---

[1] https://www.frontiersin.org/articles/10.3389/fnhum.2013.00824/full

are either of these mechanisms who we are as an identity? Are we bodies, or are our bodies vehicles for our consciousness? Beyond this, would we consider the bacteria and individual cellular components part of our body and thus part of our being? Pivot from the micro and into the macro. We are each a single cell to the celestial body of the earth, working together and separately to heal or damage our host body.

Through coming to accept the non-solitude of our existence and the temporary nature of our current reality as physical beings in the specific time frame of this life span, we may also begin to take responsibility for the way our actions, words, and thoughts impact the realities of those who surround us. It is very easy to reach a place where we are the key player within our reality; after all, subjectively speaking, you are all of existence within your reality. But when we consider the ramifications of each reality interacting with one another, we realize that only through harmony may we find a truth that is beneficial not only to others but to the self.

Our body is made up of parts, limbs, blood, organs; if we lose these parts, we may consider our body diminished, but we do not consider ourselves to be lesser beings. Through the lens of this perception, we may acknowledge that we are not our bodies.

Pull your awareness into yourself. Breathe slowly, taking note of the actions within your body that make this possible. Your diaphragm contracting and expanding, allowing your lungs to fill and empty. Feel the sensation of air entering your nostrils and exiting your mouth. How does the air feel on your lips, on your tongue?

Take a moment to do a mental inventory of the sensations. Start broadly, with the sensations of clothes, textures, or structures against your skin. Feel the weight of your corporeal self pushing against your feet or butt. Become aware of the air around you. Is it full of movement, or does it sit still and stifled all around you? Take note of the cold or the heat that permeates your space. After acknowledging and identifying the various external stimulants and obstacles to focus, dismiss them.

Focus now on those stimuli that come from within your body. Notice sore muscles, fingers or limbs that are in uncomfortable positions. Move and adjust to overcome discomfort. Understand that the signals you receive from your body come for a reason. Sometimes these aches, pings, and pains are cause for reaction. A past sensation that triggers a present doing. Sometimes they come instead from habit or psychosomatic roots. You feel antsy because you are not used to being still, or your stomach growls not from hunger but because you always eat at this time.

Take the time to discover what your body is telling you and what you are telling your body. Separate the two from each other and allow this to color your thoughts. Discover that things that seemed autonomic and beyond your control before are now within your ability to change. Your body belongs to you, and through your willpower and choices, you may take control of it.

When you are ready, allow outside stimuli back in and allow your consciousness to inhabit your body once more.

John Baltisberger

Earth

Earth, the third planet from the sun, and so far as we know, the only planet within our solar system that supports life as we currently define it. It is our home in our iteration as human consciousness in bodies, though we are constantly pushing the boundaries and seeking to expand. In this way, our goal as extent beings coincides with our goals as a species: expansion beyond the borders of established existence.

The earth provides everything from which we derive the perception of life. Air, water, plant and animal life to sustain ourselves. Depending on your view, you can view your existence on Earth as either parasitic or symbiotic. In the parasitic, we take from nature, giving nothing back but pollution, death, and destruction. In the symbiotic view, we are a part of the whole, traveling pathways well worn by purpose and necessity. Both views are equally valid, both from the personal view and the species wide view. Our current manifestations of will are certainly capable of both taking and giving back, though often the balance of these actions is thrown off by personal bias.

If we take the time to consider the structure of the Earth in relativity to our own, it becomes even easier to see ourselves not as individual beings of importance but simply cells that mirror the Earth's structure as a shadow on the wall of a cave. The planet, with veins of magma, skin of stone, and lungs of lush trees, is the perfect body, the archetypal "Adam" from which we pulled our present forms. Through the knowledge that humankind is at once the recipient of this form and the progenitor of the idea of the form, we can draw more and more from our connection to the Earth.

Ideas and concepts are powerful constructs of language and belief. Through our belief, we shape our own existence; by connecting our thoughts back to the genesis of our birth, physically and metaphysically, we connect to a deeper awareness of self and awareness of the idea of self than we can otherwise. Understand that while we use terms that disconnect us from the perceived reality, this does not disconnect the importance of the physical world or the world that is easily perceived.

Our knowledge, experience, and those things that we absorb into our idea of self come largely from the physical world around us. Though it is possible to absorb knowledge from divine and otherwise "outside" sources through meditation, prayer, and other forms of mind expanding endeavors, the majority of who we are in our current iteration is built by our interactions with the Earth as it is in our perception of today. The Earth and the physical universe contain our past, present, and future experiences in this realm and should not be ignored or dismissed out of hand. It is important to connect and disconnect. Accept the threads that tie us to the Earth even as we float free; likewise, esoteric knowledge and freedom means very little if we cannot turn around and empower our earthly lives and the lives of others with it. While we are of the Earth, and it is of us, we are not the Earth.

Begin by setting your feet on the ground — you can do this anywhere, but barefooted outside is best. Take a moment to attain some level of meditative focus. Focus on your breath as it enters you and it exits. Imagine that breath traveling through your body, expanding your lungs before it leaves. On each in breath, allow the air to travel further down your body.

Feel the air in your stomach, your bowels, your legs, and your feet. Now press beyond your feet. Imagine the breath as roots that extend past your feet and burrow into the earth. With every breath, let those roots extend further down. They push into the ground, and past the clay and rock sediment. Feel the movement of material that would impede your expansion as it is shoved aside. Feel the nutrient rich earth sustaining you as you absorb strength and vitality through your roots.

Take your time, allowing your new roots to sink deep into the dark of the earth; explore those places, feel the heat of the magma heartbeat of the molten center of the planet, and tap into the very iron core of the earth. Take that strength as your own. In this moment, there is no separation between the planet and you. This place is your body, its soul, your own.

Allow time to retract yourself from this sensation. With each breath out, allow your roots to shrink back into you, but as they absorbed the earth as they extended, they retain this strength and power. Every breath brings you closer from yourself, to yourself. Once your roots are completely gone and you are left whole, open your eyes and observe the world around you;

bask in the connection you share with the planet Earth.

John Baltisberger

Universe

It is not uncommon to hear someone who is focused on meditation or a zen existence to talk about being one with the universe. But what does this mean? They may mean their corporeal form is crafted from the same matter and importance as all other physical bodies in the universe, made of stars. Or perhaps they refer to their spiritual self being connected with the spirits of other people and animals. Whatever the meaning, it is important to remember that such a statement is both subjectively true and absolutely filled with hubris all at once.

From a cosmic point of view, there is no difference between us and any other object within creation. We are of such insignificance that we blend into the non-importance of our surroundings. In this way, all things in the universe are one, nothing having any more importance than any other.

Mentally, we are unable to grasp, as physical intellectual creatures, the vastness of our world. It is difficult to truly understand the number of people within a major city, let alone the animals, insects, and billions upon billions of microscopic life. When we expand this area to a large geography, the numbers grow staggeringly large. The possibility of comprehending all of the life within any given territory, let alone "being connected with all life in the universe," is something to be approached with some skepticism.

What I believe most mean is that through some sort of spiritual practice, they have found a sort of peace. A balance between their asynchronous existence as physical manifestations and spiritual beings. This feeling of peace can indeed feel like a connection to the universe at large, a sensation similar to a puzzle piece sliding into the correct place.

It is taught that we are like a speck

of dust, but that simultaneously, the universe was crafted for us. This impossible juxtaposition is easiest to understand when we understand the subjective nature of truth and reality. As stated from the cosmic perspective, we are next to nothing; it is also true that we do not view the world from a cosmic perspective, but from a human one. It is from this mental space that we must judge our connection to the greater universe around us.

Walking the path of seeking connection is laudable. Understanding both our own insignificance and that we are not alone in this reality allows us to do greater good and act with greater compassion within our incarnation as human beings. This in turn increases our ability to connect with our immediate surroundings. It is important, of course, to remember that physical interaction is not the only path towards interaction and interconnectivity. In this digital age, we may connect and do good works through many different means, and connection has never meant such a variety of actions before now.

We may seek connection while understanding the sheer enormity of the task we set before ourselves. By understanding the feeling and the reality as being separate things, we may also understand that though, through peace, we may feel connected, we are not the universe.

Take several moments to slip into your meditation ritual. Push your awareness out from your body to explore your immediate surroundings. You may do this with your eyes or in your mind's eye. Explore the air in the room. Become aware of it and its subtle movements. Tune your ears to every sound—you don't need to identify them, just be aware of them. If you begin to grow overwhelmed, simply pull your awareness back to a comfortable space and focus on your breathing again.

As you are ready, push further, consider a larger radius than your immediate surroundings. The universe contains all physical things, and, therefore, all physical things are part of the universe. The ground you are on, the air that you breathe, you yourself are all a part of the universe. Allow this knowledge to infuse you with the enormity of your importance. The universe would literally be lesser if not for your existence.

Empowered by the knowledge of your place within the greater mechanics of reality, wrap your senses around all that you have expanded out to and pull your awareness and connection to the surroundings into yourself. As there is no difference from a macro scale between you and these things you have subsumed, you may forgo connection and realize that you are truly one with your surroundings and with the universe as a whole.

Secure in this knowledge, allow the feeling of connection to apply to your own body. Feel your body as if it were the air. As if it were created from the stone and earth of the ground. Feel the presence of wildlife and sense the world through their senses. When you are prepared to, let these sensations go and return to your breath. Breathe in the universe, breathe out the universe.

Open your eyes a separate entity that is at once one with the universe.

Oneness

Look deeper at the concept of oneness. Out of all the concepts that are taught in an effort to transcend human consciousness, this can be the most dangerous to one's mental health. When coming into the understanding that there is no true distinction between your consciousness and the universal consciousness, many fall into a paradox. This paradox exists in two ways.

First, those who have achieved this base level of esoteric understanding separate their lives into a before and after understanding. This, of course, is a false dichotomy, the person's reality has not changed, only their subjective view of it. Even concepts of before and after must fall away for a true understanding of oneness.

This is an artifact of an ego that must be avoided at all costs. Those who have glimpsed the esoteric truth of oneness often believe they have grasped and absorbed the concepts with their whole consciousness, where they have instead only considered the topic on a cerebral level without an emotional or deeper connection.

Second, many take on the concept with oneness and then also disconnect themselves from others who have not made that connection. Oneness is a radical concept, you must be one not only with positive and pleasant vibes, you are also one with the darkness. This can be difficult to swallow, especially if you follow a theological path for your esoterica. Once you accept oneness, you must connect that not only to the highest highs but the darkest and most horrid lows. With this connection must come empathy and disgust. We must empathize with the pain that not only caused our actions but were caused by our actions. We must be disgusted not only by the harm we cause but the harm that begot it.

You cannot embrace oneness and then feel anger towards someone else for their behavior, it is your own behavior. To truly be one is to understand that there are no separators; personal responsibility and blame become meaningless as all actions and consequences begin and end with the self. This knowledge can be extremely destructive to the self, as the self loses meaning in the flow of all things. The weight of the world, all of creation, rests on your shoulders. Every action is entwined and changes the reality of the moment and all of the moments that follow.

Through the understanding of the immense importance of our actions, we begin to behave in a way that will increase the net positivity that is present in each moment we are aware of. Through our heightened and expanded view of the world around what we mistakenly call ourselves, we work at increasing the impact of our actions throughout the world in a way that will not only increase our individual happiness but the universal good (as we understand it).

The Subjective Truth of the Esoteric Self

Bring your attention inward, focus first on your breath, and then allow that awareness to slip away. Be aware of where you are, of the space you occupy. Expand this awareness to beyond, becoming aware of where you end and begin. With your senses, your awareness expands far beyond your body. Your senses are part of your identity and therefore you are what you sense and observe.

There are things beyond your observation; these things are no different than those things you do, therefore, there is no difference between you and them, there is no them. Understanding oneness goes far beyond what we may observe as temporal single conscious entities; we must fight against the biology and mechanics of our animal forms. Focus your mind on the concept of oneness. Grapple with the idea of no separation. Forgive yourself for being unable to fully grasp the concepts. Understand that oneness, while a hidden truth behind the veil of perception, is no simple thing to understand.

Forgive yourself, and with the cerebral understanding that there is no separation between you and others, forgive others. Understand there is no difference between yourself and an event; forgive events. Understand that while you are not defined by any emotional state, you are an ever-shifting continuum of connected emotional and physical events. Understand that the self is all of this. Let each breath carry awareness and forgiveness outward into the rest of you.

Nothingness

Here we come to the ultimate truth, one grasped at by many esoteric and occult pathways. Nothing is objectively true.

Nothing is often terrifying to people. The concept exists in the physical universe, each object around us exists in its current form as a collection of atoms arranged in a certain order with a certain connection, but over time, this changes. On a long enough scale, not only are we born of star dust, we return to it as well. Nothing waits for us at the end. Nothing is in the dark, and the light itself is Nothing. Our hopes, dreams, our thoughts and our emotions all amount to Nothing.

But is Nothing something to be scared of? Some nihilists will postulate that if Nothing is true and Nothing exists, then all effort and thought are ultimately meaningless. Others would take the freedom of Nothingness in another direction, assigning importance only to actions and thoughts, with the non-existence of material objects at the front of mind. And it is true that the subjective truth of Nothing can overwhelm a person; it can, if allowed, eat away at the psyche and personality of those contemplating the very concept.

It does not have to subsume you.

When looking at the concept of Nothingness, we grasp at concepts beyond what our current temporal physical existence is truly capable of understanding. We think of Nothingness as the dark, or as a white space, but it is filled with air and color and shadows and time. To truly contemplate nothing is to empty the mind of even the smallest concept of existence. It is to be pulled out of our four-dimensional lives and find anchor in the true divinity that may only exist outside all other concepts.

When we attempt to subjectively define the divine, we attach concepts that are familiar and comforting to it. We allow our own temporal and physical existence to intrude on and corrupt divinity with notions that are entirely part of something tied to desire, fear, and hope. By coloring divinity with these human emotions, we begin to view divinity as something reactive, something that comes from a place of judgment and severity and often cruelty. However, if we allow for nothing to be holy and accept that nothing has divine providence, we can then understand that our concepts of right, wrong, and all judgments are not mandated from the divine but part of the human experience and dichotomy of power.

The phrase "everything is permitted" does not mean you are free of your consequences, or from the judgment of people, but rather that any guilt or fear you have assigned yourself as being from the divine is ultimately from yourself. By understanding the nothingness as being the divine, we may divorce ourselves from the sorrow of Draconian thoughts and self-hurt we have been conditioned to feel, freeing us to do and be good as we define it without fear of reprisal from a deity defined by others' fears and guilts.

This is a tightrope; some will use this as an excuse to become monstrous individuals, others will throw every tangible object and relationship away to fully bask in nothingness. But by walking the center path along the tightrope, we may understand the twin importance of the subjective reality of human morals and our freedom from divine judgment. We may exist in a way that brings harmony, joy, and peace to our present temporal existence.

Sit or stand still. The word holy in Hebrew is "kadosh". This means singular or unique. As you are still, consider what is holy to you. What is unique? What fills you with awe? Perhaps it is the ocean or sunsets. Perhaps it is a book or even a relationship. Consider for a moment if these things exude judgment. Consider for a moment if these things are truly unique or if their holiness is simply assigned to them due to other connotations attached from your own experience.

As you consider the subjectivity of your concepts of holiness, peel away those things you know to be internal from the eternal. Strip every human notion of divinity away and you will be left with Nothing. Understand that Nothing is not the absence of all, but the absence of anything you are capable of understanding in your current incarnation.

Contemplate what this means for you, for the absolute truth at the center of this reality to be nothing and yet for the subjective truth all around you to be filled with physical, emotional, and conceptual things. The concrete takes so much of your attention every moment, bask in the absence of the concrete, the absence of obligation.

Grapple with non-meaning; consider what the nothingness is to you, what it means for you. Understand that even these meanings are subjective interpretations created from your internal dialog and have no true bearing on the nothingness. Understanding that your fears are internal frees you to dismiss them as you come to terms with them.

Open your eyes, face the world with a core of peace inside you.

The Subjective Truth of the Esoteric Self

Rituals

Sitting

Sitting is by and large the most common and the most widely accepted form meditation takes. This format is perhaps the most welcoming and forgiving to new practitioners of meditation. Though, it can also be an impediment at the same time. By seeing meditation as sitting, you may feel like it is meaningless to those who spend most if not all their time sitting for work or hobbies. Or it may add another "to-do" to an already hectic day.

For the first issue, when getting started, feel freed to change the way you sit. If you are always sitting at a desk, instead find a pillow and sit on the floor, or sink into a recliner. If you are trying to work your meditative practice into before or after sleep, try sitting on the edge of your bed. It is always useful to create a separate space for separate activities. By doing so, you prepare your mental state, you signal to your brain and therefore to your body that this is time for meditation, for calmness.

For the second issue, understand that while it does add another item to your to-do list, think of it not as something you have to do, but rather a time out from your obligations. Treat your meditation as a mini-Sabbath, a disruption away from work. Much like sitting in a way that is unique to your meditative practice, cutting your practice away from the have-to-dos will assist you in making it different and an escape from the roadblocks to your peace and health.

Find a comfortable place, or make a place more comfortable to you. Though the mental image of a monk meditating in an icy-storm, immune to the pain or discomfort, is very popular, your goal in starting your practice should not be to withstand anything at all. Rather, by making yourself comfortable, you minimize the number of things that can distract you from your thoughts. If you are in a cold place, wrap yourself in a blanket as you sit. If it is hot, turn on a fan. Make sure you are in a position that you can sustain for your full practice.

Let your body dictate that as well. You will find that, at first, you may only be able to sit still for a minute; this will build the longer you have consistent meditative rituals. It is important that you do not judge yourself based on how long you can comfortably meditate, nor judge yourself if you become distracted by stray thoughts and other daydreams. While these things do intrude on the meditative state, creating a moment and a mindfulness that is free of judgment is just as important as any of the other concepts within this book.

Once you are in a comfortable place and sitting comfortably, let your body rest naturally; don't worry about sitting straight or where your hands are. Rather, let your hands rest in a natural position—at your side, on your legs, or in your lap. If you feel uncomfortable at any time, allow for those small adjustments. As you grow in your practice, you will be able to dismiss those thoughts of discomfort, seeing them as momentary twinges in a moment you can transcend.

Now that you are seated comfortably, allow your eyes to close and consider the stillness of your body. Imagine that the entire universe is this moment, this place. You and the surface you are resting on are the only things that exist. Be aware of your body, the sensations you can feel against your skin and hair, the movement of air, the stretch across your chest as you breathe. As you become aware of each sensation, acknowledge its existence and then dismiss it.

Allow your mind to focus solely on your breath. As other thoughts intrude, acknowledge their existence and bring your thoughts back to maintaining even breaths. When you breathe in, relax the diaphragm and expand the lungs. On your exhale, pay attention to the natural length of the exhale. Pay attention to the way the lungs deflate and the diaphragm tightens. Paying attention to this process will fill your mental space, taking room away from other thoughts.

In this moment, your entire being is your breath. Life sustaining, existing in each moment, either in your control or as an autonomic process outside and independent of your thoughts. By taking control and paying close attention to your breath, you may let other things slip from your control and attention, giving yourself a moment's respite from perceived external obligations and stresses.

Visualization

Throughout this book, we have used visualization within our meditative practice; this has allowed us to view concepts both concrete and abstract within our mind's eye. But why do we use this form of practice? Visualization is one of the most important tools in meditative practice because it allows us to focus our intention. Our minds wander, this is as true a fact as we are able to establish in a wholly subjective reality. Through the use of visuals, we call into our mind's eye, we are able to keep our subconscious attention much easier.

Many forms of visualization involve walking through a forest path or enjoying nature. Some give color and substance to the breath or direct cooling energy to different parts of the body. These forms of active visualization, in which there is movement, are often used to help calm and reduce anxiety. However, visualization can play many roles in meditation. Much like a mantra, a visualization acts as a totem for your intention. Something for you to wrap your awareness around that pulls your conscious and subconscious self towards the subject or subjects you wish to focus on.

You might focus on the image the Sanskrit word for Aum or the Christian cross, or a tree whose branches reach as high as the roots dig low. Each symbol brings with it different thoughts and contemplations. And though I use religious or spiritual imagery here, this is not a limitation you need concern yourself with. If you wanted to meditate in order to further a creative endeavor, you could choose a symbol central to the art you are creating and meditate upon it, or you may even concentrate on an image that connects to the feel of what you are hoping to achieve.

You can also side step all of this and work through visualization practices that include photos of those you love, if you are looking to increase your joy and love.

You may also practice visualization with words. Here I will describe a particularly Jewish form of word visualization:

We begin by seeing the tetragrammaton before us in black flames on white flames. This four-letter word is a special name for divinity, Once the entire word is before us, we focus on one letter at a time. First, the Yod, a small curved letter, reminiscent of a gust of wind or a small ember. We can think of words that begin with Yod. What do those words mean to us? How do they tie back to the prospect of divinity within and outside of us? You may spend a minute on each letter of the tetragrammaton or may in fact spend multiple sessions on each letter. The goal is not to complete the holy name, but rather to find completeness in your practice.

While the above is couched in terms of divinity and holiness and Jewish practice, it is important to remember this tool could be used for any word.

Begin with the word Kindness. Notice the colors you associate with the word; are they pastels or bright? Are they solid color or patterns? Allow your mind to be filled with the letter K—Kindness, kisses, kittens, koalas—focus on what the letter k means to you and what images are associated with it. Move through each letter of the word, allowing the connotation of loving kindness to wash over you as you allow each letter to morph into images you associate with it. Take as much or as little time with every letter as you need.

Remember that it's not the word that matters but your associations with it.

Chanting

Chanting is an effective way to occupy your conscious mind, filtering out your mundane thoughts and focusing them instead on an intention. One can chant in any language, or simply with sound. The most recognizable chant would be the so called "universal sound" om or aum. This chant, most famously used in Buddhist meditation, is ascribed with countless benefits, most of a completely subjective and superstitious nature. It is said to promote self-healing, purify the environment around you, and even improve your eyesight. Of course, the only true benefit we are concerning ourselves with is the benefit to your conscious and subconscious self through the use of meditation.

Aum is a fantastic tool for a beginner of chanting meditation because you may effortlessly include it in your exhalation. You simply open your mouth and vocalize as you breathe out, continuing until you no longer have breath to vocalize, then it is time to breathe in. It will assist you in ensuring you take full, deep breaths, as well as occupying your thoughts. For some, this will be enough to ensure a peaceful meditation, especially when combined with visualization. Many will concentrate or visualize the Tibetan symbol for the universal sound below.

It can also be useful to wrap affirmations into your meditative practice as a chanted mantra. Through positive reinforcement, you may shape the way your conscious mind thinks and forge new neural pathways to achieve belief and self-actualization that you found difficult before.

The Subjective Truth of the Esoteric Self

With affirmations, it is important to follow a few rules: speak in the first person, use positive statements, and speak in the present. You may chant. "I am happy with myself." Or, "I am free of addiction." While affirmations are not a magic spell that will change the world or yourself without action, they are useful for setting your mind towards a specific intention. Often, the first person who must be convinced of any truth, and the one who must be convinced before change can take place, is the self. Through altering your subjective view of your own person, you begin to effect change in the subjective truth that is presented to the world.

You may also integrate prayer into your meditative practice through chanting. Prayer and meditation are often linked together and considered in the same thought. Quiet contemplation sometimes, in repose, does share much in spirit with meditation. However, through the use of a chanting mantra, we can focus our intention and strengthen our own faith, sometimes finding comfort, beauty, and a relief to emotional, physical, or spiritual pain through the connection of our subjective self to our subjective understanding of divinity. Below are a few chants one might use in religious mantra.

- **Catholic:** *"Gloria Patri, et Filio, et Spiritui Sancto. Sicut erat in principio, et nunc, et semper, et in saecula saeculorum"* Glory to the father, the son, and the holy spirit. As it was in the beginning, is now and ever shall be.
- **Jewish:** *"Elohai neshama shenata ta be, te hora he"* HaShem, the soul you have given me, she is pure.
- **Muslim:** *"Rabbe zidni ilma"* O Lord, increase my knowledge.
- **Buddhist:** *"Nam myoho renge kyo"* I devote myself to blossom like a lotus"
- **Protestant:** *"For if ye forgive men their trespasses, your heavenly Father will also forgive*

The Subjective Truth of the Esoteric Self

you."
- Hindu: *"Asato ma sad gamaya, tamaso ma jyotir gamaya, mrtyor mamrtam gamaya."* From the unreal, lead me to the real, from the dark, lead me to the light, from death, lead me to immortality.
- Humanist/Atheist: *"I am human, I am worthy of love and capable of sharing love outward."*

The world is filled with faiths, religions, and languages, such that it would be impossible to give even the smallest percentage of examples for the various ways people connect to the divine. Though I tried to include some of the largest belief systems and languages here, do not for one moment believe that these are the established or accepted pathways to meditative contemplation; rather, your chant must resonate with you. Finding a chant that resonates along your belief, culture, and language will be the most meaningful and assist you in achieving your goals far more than adopting one that is foreign or alien.

Sit and practice your breathing. When you are breathing fully and fully invested in your breathing, begin vocalization. On each exhale, intone the sound "Aum." It does not have to be loud, it does not need to be pronounced perfectly; instead, allow your attention to be on simply making the sound. Feel the vibration in your throat and chest. Allow it to envelop your attention. The meaning of the words is less important than the sound that echoes through your chest and outward into the world. Your words and intention move the air; they cause further vibrations in the atoms of the objects they touch and those that touch those objects and so on ad infinitum. Through the sound of your mantra, you manifest your being throughout all of creation.

Yoga/Tai Chi

Yoga is a common means of meditative practice which combines movement, breathing, stretching, and mindfulness. While often used as a means of fitness and exercise, it is very possible to also exercise your mind and soul at the same moment as your body. While yoga can be extremely involved and take a lifetime to master, it is possible to incorporate a small yoga practice into your life almost immediately. I recommend keeping your meditative and yoga practice separate to start, and then merge them as you become comfortable with each.

Yoga and Tai Chi are valuable as both exercise and as meditative techniques, working in similar ways to chanting. By occupying the mind with movement, you can hedge out other thoughts, focusing instead on being mindful of that one moment in time, in tune with the subjective reality of your physical incarnation. These forms of exercise focus on slow, deliberate movements, which are often at odds with our daily activities and movements. The separation of sudden movement from deliberate movement can be very jarring if you are not careful. But through using this technique, you can separate the moments of your life that are frantic from those you wish to be still.

Included is an image of various yoga positions, but do not feel overwhelmed by the plethora of options, we will look at one simple sequence that I find useful.

As we work through this sequence, remember to breathe, a full breath in and a full breath out. This serves three purposes. By taking full, deep breaths, you carry oxygen to the muscles you are stretching, which aids the body in its natural healing process as well as maximizing the health benefits of your stretches. By taking full, deep breaths, you will find it easier to maintain a relaxed state that is helpful for both exercise and meditation. By continuing to breathe, you continue your current incarnation in this temporal existence. By this same token, make every movement deliberate and slow, with purpose.

First, start with your feet shoulder width apart, standing straight with your arms at your side. Slowly reach up, keeping your feet flat on the ground, with knees slightly bent, reach above your head; look up as though enjoying the sun on your face. Hold this stretch for three counts. Then, allow your arms and hands to float down beside you, and start with your head bend. Try to imagine each vertebra taking its turn bending as you reach down in front of you. Allow yourself to hang over. Look forward and then allow your head to drop back down; if possible, grab your ankles or calves and gently pull yourself to them. Feel the stretch throughout your back; breathe into that stretch. Straighten your back to stand upright once more.

Bending one leg, step back with the other in a half lunge. Spread your arms wide and slowly twist your body while inhaling deeply; on the exhale, untwist back to front. Repeat the process for each side. Move then so you are lying on your stomach, legs straight; put your palms flat on the ground and lift your upper body off the ground. Hold this position as you breathe in and out. When you are finished, lift your butt, bend your knees, and push back so you are curled over your legs with your arms once more stretched out ahead of you and your face down. Feel the stretch in your lower back. When you are ready, lift your head slowly and move to sit.

When you are comfortable combining mindful movement with mindful thought, move through your preferred form of meditation. Allow yourself to first fully embrace the movement, focusing solely on your body as you purposefully move through path of various forms. When your body has fully embraced movement as a part of its being, allow yourself to consider the feelings of your muscles as they interact. As one leg moves, which muscles move within your hip? How do they interact with one another to allow the full range of your possible movement?

Consider the way your body's movement mirrors the movement of objects through time. In each instance you are still, it is only when viewed through the fourth dimension of linear temporal existence that we achieve movement. If you were to pause in one position, consider whether or not that position is truly held in "stillness." Your breath, your heartbeat, the synapses firing, all constitute a type of movement outside of your control.

Consider the way our bodies move: we will it to do so, and it does. But what conscious thought do we set to the contraction of muscle groups or the relaxing of tendons? In reality, although we often perceive ourselves to control our bodies and our selves, our conscious efforts are as autonomic as those we have no conscious control over.

Consider the paradox of your uncontrolled body as you move through your controlled motions; allow it to suffuse your intention towards embracing the chaos that orders our lives.

Walking

Often when I suggest walking as a valid form of meditation, people are surprised. But the fact is true that, as a species, we are often too hurried without our perceived importance of time. It is sometimes difficult, if not impossible, to work a meditative practice in with our rushed lives. We feel the need to make time for cooking, eating, exercise, work, creative endeavors, sleep, and romantic or procreative endeavors. Only once all of this is accomplished can we wrap our minds around the dire need for stillness.

But we are not our bodies. Our minds and our bodies do not have to be in perfect stillness together to achieve something of peace. Instead, we may find the opportunity to "go on autopilot" to allow our autonomic senses and motor skills to take control as we allow our mind, untethered from tasks, to float free. Even this is a rare gift for most.

Most people listen to music or gaze at their phone as they walk, unwilling to allow mindfulness to seep into the moment.

But a walk is the perfect moment to become mindful. You are surrounded by sensory communication from the world around you in that moment. If you take your time to actually be aware of your surroundings, you will notice colors, sounds, and sensations that are often lost in the background static of our busy minds. Though often in meditative practice our goal is to turn inward and be aware of the internal, a walk is a time to reverse this and allow your mind to explore aspects of the world around you that you often ignore. Observe the leaves and grass during the summer, make out shapes in and distinction in the clouds during an overcast winter day, take special note of the details on cars, spots where the paint has been scratched and rust is setting in.

While we are almost always "aware"

of these details, it is rare that they take the forefront in our thoughts. As we have spoken about in other parts of this book, sometimes meditation is less about introspection and more about separating your practice from the other temporal instances in your day. Through becoming more aware of the details that surround you during your walk, you may place your mind in a different space, one that is more aware of the world around you and less aware of the minute and subjective stresses we find ourselves experiencing.

As you walk, take a few moments, pay attention to your body. You propel yourself forward without the thoughts of movement, your motions are both conscious and subconscious. Allow your mind to settle on your breathing. If you are breathing hard, slow down, keep a pace that allows you to inhale and exhale fully as you walk. Pay attention to how your breathing now differs from when your body is not in motion.

As your attention drifts from your breathing, look around you. Take note of the feeling of the air and wind on your skin, how the time of day effects the temperature and humidity. What are the light sources, and how are they interacting with the natural and man-made world around you? Consider how the colors of the world around you are different at different times of day, how each moment the very nature of the world is subjective to not only the physical incarnation of the viewer but the temporal moment that being exists in.

Through your walking, allow your mind to touch on those things that make up the world around you; when you find your mind turning to internal stress or matters outside of your immediate surroundings, gently correct your thoughts. Dismissing those that do not pertain to immediacy, walk in peace and in that subjectively present moment.

Smudging

Smudging is a practice most commonly encountered in new age circles where hippies and neo-pagan witchcraft intersect. But the truth is that smudging is not a new practice and has its roots in truly ancient customs. Into antiquity, you could find Israelites and other ancient people burning herbs, meats, and other objects to create a pleasant smelling smoke, offering the scent up to spirits, angels, and even deities. If you walk into any natural grocers or store that caters to new age clientele, you'll find at least one shelf of bundles of dried sage for use in smudging.

I would like, however, to encourage you to grow and dry your own white sage. By doing so, you will enjoy the benefits of gardening, which can in and of itself be soothing and meditative, and it will also be better for the environment and for your own health in the long run. Through growing your own, you will avoid pesticides or engaging with a company that sources product unethically.

If you look up smudging or do any research, you'll be inundated with the hundreds of ways it supposedly benefits you. You will purify yourself, dispel negative energy or demons. People claim it can heal you, make you smarter, or stronger, that it will help you sleep. I will make none of those claims; I only claim it can be a useful tool for meditative practice.

Smudging for our purposes combines several other methods of meditation we have spoken of before. Your eyes can lock on the rising smoke, and you can allow yourself to get lost in the shifting images that exist there. You can move from room to room, "smudging" each room, walking and breathing in the scent as you focus your intention; and you can chant a mantra as you do, combining movement, sound, and visuals, all in one powerful concentration of intention.

In this case, the smoke rising from your smudge acts as the totem that you imbue with your thoughts; the mantra you chant works to focus the thoughts that you imbue into the visuals of the smoke. This can be done walking or sitting, as you desire, but much like incense, the smell and act of burning the smudge may act as a signal to your conscious mind that this is a time for calm contemplation. Through the regular use of this method, just the smell of your smudge will be enough to move your mind towards a more meditative state.

Light your sage bundle, allowing it to burn for a moment before blowing out the flames. Watch the smoke drift upward. Consider the way the air in the room manipulates the smoke as it rises. Do you see shapes in the smoke? If so, consider what your mind is setting into the smoke; are the symbols or images easy to explain? Are they confusing? Every image you see within the smoke is placed there by your subconscious mind.

Interpret your own will as the smoke rises.

The Subjective Truth of the Esoteric Self

Obstacles to Peace

Anxiety

The first step is to change our syntax. Do not say "I am anxious," as the anxiety is not your identity; rather say, "I am experiencing the feeling of anxiety in this moment." Anxiety is usually a symptom of some other cause, but not necessarily. Anxiety is the feeling that something has or will soon go wrong. It is the feeling of looming disaster. As such, anxiety is a symptom of living not within the present but the future. As we discuss in the section of the future, this can be addressed by remembering that the future only exists as a subjective understanding of time and the physical overlap of energy and awareness.

Consider also non-emotional reasons for anxiety. Often, excessive tiredness or hunger may provoke anxiety. Our physical form demands sustenance and rest, and the absence of these will trigger your fight or flight. But with no present visible threat, this is translated by our conscious minds as dread. Once you have ascertained that the cause of your anxiety is not a need, you may address it.

In any time and place, anxiety must be addressed before one can explore a peaceful existence. Through the understanding that your anxiety exists due to placing importance on events that have not yet happened, or on events that happened in the past, you may understand that your anxiety is rooted not in objective and rational thought, but rather a self-harming subjective view of not only the self but of the world in which you find yourself.

Focus on this aspect of the anxiety; do not think on it as irrational, but consider what is rational. It is rational to understand your discomfort is internal. It is rational to understand your anxiety is neither deadly nor harmful to your physical body in and of itself. Though this will not banish the anxiety, it allows you to understand its presence and to move past it.

It will be tempting to move, to siphon off your anxious energy through momentum. We would instead recommend sitting still. As anxiety grows and we are not harmed, we will realize that, as in all things, the subject sensation of anxiety is submissive to our esoteric and true selves.

Sit and take stock of your body. Your muscles, your skin, your hands, and limbs. Take a moment to slow your breathing, ensure your breathing is full. Taking the time to fully exhale and then fully inhale, allow your lungs to expand, taking in oxygen which will flood throughout your body, healing damage to muscles and allowing them to relax if possible.

Once you have fully invested yourself in breathing, consider the feeling of anxiety as being separate from you. It is not a part of you or a piece of you, but a thing that you have taken within your being and, having done so, have the power to excise as well. Visualize the anxiety as a colored smoke that escapes from you with every exhale.

As you inhale, take in clean, pure air; and with each exhale, see the vessel of your physical incarnation empty itself of the tainted anxiety. See it leave your body and dissipate in the air around you, lifted by the wind and utterly unmade by your intention.

Anger

The first step is to change our syntax. Do not say "I am angry," as the rage is not your identity; rather say, "I am experiencing the feeling of anger in this moment." Anger is an incredibly dangerous emotional state to find oneself in. When angry, we tend to act rashly, we make poor decisions, we hurt those we would rather not hurt.

Anger is self-sustaining. We latch onto our rage and fabricate entire arguments and slights in our heads which bear the weight of real rage, we see the world through eyes that victimize the self. We put ourselves in a place of righteous fury; we are right, they are wrong. In this state, it is too easy to slip into a thought pattern of separation, no longer capable of seeing the evidence of oneness, but instead setting up a chess board where we take on all comers with our superiority. It is in this frame of mind that we can do incredible damage to our psyche, our friendships, and through acts of destruction or distraction, to our own physical selves.

Anger, especially self-righteous anger, feels good. We feel validated and powerful, but this is an illusion created by the conscious mind. Anger is a mask—loud and brash and obnoxious—over the true emotion you are experiencing: fear. Anger exists only in order to hide the fear that is being experienced by the subconscious.

When we experience anger, it is due to a fear of inadequacy, a fear of the unknown. Our first step when we experience anger, then, is to discover what we are afraid of.

Look at the so called "external" triggers for your anger; what about them brings you fear? Do you fear they do not or will not respect you? Do you fear they will take advantage of you? Or is your anger a fear of a lack of control of your surroundings? A fear of ineptitude? As you understand that those outward stimuli that are sparking anger are only a perceived externalization of what is truly an internal fear, you may begin the work of overcoming anger.

I recommend walking or yoga during meditation to overcome experiencing anger. Your body has entered fight or flight, and moving will relieve your need for action as you work through the mental blocks.

Start by breathing steadily. As in most instances of heightened emotional state, we forget to breathe or breathe shallowly. Focus on taking slow, calm breaths, hold your breath for a count between each inhale and each exhale. Allow for an outward calm to seep into you and become an internalized calm.

Consider the trigger for your anger; understand why it has caused fear within you. Now consider what good this fear does. Will the fear keep you safe, or hinder your safety? In most cases, calm and measured action will be a better answer than brash action. Consider why this trigger affects you so deeply, consider other things in your life that may have led you to being more prone to reaction now. As in all things, you are not solely one experience or one emotional state.

When you feel you have identified the source of your fear, or the conglomerate circumstances that led to this emotional experience, acknowledge them as being part of your temporal and physical life, but dismiss them as controlling factors.

John Baltisberger

Depression

Depression can have many causes. First and foremost, it is important to understand that depression can be caused by a chemical imbalance with our central nervous system. While the body and the brain are but temporary vehicles and aspects of our entire being, we must contend with the reality that medical science has set forth. While sunshine, exercise, and other "healthy activities" can help with non-clinical depression, as can meditation, if you need help from therapists, psychologists, or pharmaceuticals, do not see this as a failure on your part. Do not see this as a weakness or a short-falling. Get the help you need as you need it

Here, we are not talking about clinical depression, but the sadness and depression that can be overcome through change in habits and thinking. The first step is to change our syntax. Do not say "I am depressed" or "I am sad," as the depression or sadness is not your identity; rather say, "I am experiencing the feeling of sadness/despair/depression in this moment." Of all the emotional states, sadness is the one we are most likely to allow to define us. It is a massive overbearing wave of emotions that can sap our will. While I would love to sit down and tell you that using a smudging ritual while holding this book will cure your sadness, I will not.

Instead, let us try to look at sadness from different angles. First, remember that you are an infinite being, capable of a full range of emotional states, born of the same energy and substance as the sun, the Earth, and all celestial bodies. Sadness is present, but it is an aspect of a prism of the emotional spectrum.

Often, sadness comes from another time: sadness from the past is often grief, sadness that comes from the future is often greed or loneliness. I invite you to examine what is truly making you sad and then look to those parts of the book that best address that issue.

A final word on depression: while subjectively we often feel alone, isolated in our pain, the esoteric truth shows us as all connected, all beings experiencing the full brunt of the emotional spectrum; you are not alone, there are others experiencing sadness, and there are others who care about you.

As sadness has other root causes, often the best action is to contemplate the root cause of your sadness. If it is something you can address immediately, do that, and then meditate on how the temporary experience of sadness allowed you to address an issue. If it is not something that you are capable of changing on your own, instead reflect on peace.

Take your smudge and direct your attention to the smoke rising. Walk from room to room chanting a mantra, allowing your mind to be fully invested not in an emotional state but in the action of the repeated mantra and smudging. As you repeat a mantra of loving kindness, allow love to radiate from you for friends, family, and activities that bring you joy; as you radiate joy, allow that happiness to come back into you.

If sadness will not be dispersed in this way, sit and watch your smudge smoke burn, allow yourself to cry if need be. Do not force happiness, but do know that you are experiencing a temporary emotion and you are not confined to being sad permanently.

Greed

The first step is to change our syntax. Do not say "I am greedy" or "I am envious," as the greed and envy is not your identity; rather say, "I am experiencing the feeling of greed/envy in this moment." Greed is the desire for external things, usually things we cannot have. Often this is physical things such as money or food, but can just as easily manifest as lust or even an overwhelming desire for respect. In any of these cases, greed is an aspect of living in the future. Desiring to come into the ownership of whatever it is you crave while ignoring what you have now is certainly forward facing misery. Sometimes, it is reversed, and we lament over something we no longer have, though this often manifests not as greed but as grief.

Emotions are messy in this way, as they tend to not come in one shade but an over cast ocean of varying feelings and responses. But much like an actual ocean, we may rise above the waves. When it comes to greed, consider the object of your desire; is it something you actually need? Likely not, most things we desire exist well outside the limited resources needed to sustain life. So the next question is, would that object create for you a better life?

At first glance, the answer is yes. Your subjective conscious brain seeks the object, why else would you want it if it would not improve the quality of your life? But as we have already explored, the self is mostly an illusion. Your conscious brain seeks material things not because they will actually improve your temporal existence but because they distract from other emotional pains or personal insecurities. To grow fully into the esoteric self, we must abandon the self-deceit of hiding from our insecurities. Understanding the truth of nothingness at the center of reality, we can grapple with the concept that material belongings are simply an aspect of our subjective understanding of our own lives. This does not mean living as a pauper or hermit, but it does mean recognizing when a desire for an object is simply the desire to block out other emotions.

Begin your motion meditation practice, whether it is yoga, tai chi, walking, or some other form of meditation. Focus first on your breathing. Consider the act of desiring something outside of your needs. There need not be any guilt associated with it, simply acknowledge that you want something. Consider what in your life has sparked this desire.

Allowing your breath to come steadily, consider the places in your life you feel fulfilled. With each breath out, focus your intention on being content with where your life is in this exact moment. Allow that contentment to fill you. Understand that no matter how much you attain, there will always be more to attain, there is no rush.

The Subjective Truth of the Esoteric Self

By accepting that physical things are simply objects that only offer temporary distraction from the true pursuit of wholeness, we may see past our current desire and focus on the present that we wish to exist in.

Grief

First, let us address that grief is a natural response to loss. There is nothing wrong, shameful, or embarrassing about experiencing the emotion of grief. Loss can often be a profound disruption in our temporal life; the fractures that we feel stretch past our conscious and deep into the core of our true being. Grief is unique in that it exists in all temporal places at once. We sit in the new hurt of the recent loss, our grief forever colors our memories of the past with bittersweet sadness, and we look forward to a world in which our loss is permanent.

How then can we find peace in the midst of grief? The first step is to remember that you are not your thoughts. As in all things, grief is an emotion resonance that we experience, but it does not define us, and it only shapes us in the ways we allow it to. Every consciousness deals with grief differently; some surround themselves with friends, others delve into solitude. There are those who engage in destructive activities and those who do nothing, unable to rouse themselves from bed during their intense grief.

The goal of some meditative practices is to overcome all physical and emotional roadblocks on the path to peace and enlightenment; for others, we seek health and calmness. Through meditation, we are able to focus only on the here and now; instead of viewing our grief through the lens of the full breadth of time and space, we can sit with what is happening in the here and now. Focusing on the oneness, the lack of distinction between yourself and others, as well as from one moment to the next may give you comfort. While it is a common notion that the memory of your loved ones live on with you and is therefore never truly gone, it is a subjective truth that through our contact with others we mix and absorb their essence, we are a conglomerate of experiences that include those we have lost. In this way, people live on through immortality even once their temporal incarnation in this physical plane ceases.

The lessons and experiences we have had irrevocably color how we present ourselves to the rest of reality, and through our own colored actions and thoughts, we color those around us in turn. In this way, our lives and our experiences continue in an outward as ripples in experiential resonance that changes the entire world.

Let us work with the mantra "I am here" or, in Hebrew, "Hineyni". Sit and focus on the phrase, "I am here, I am here in this moment, I am here in this place." I am here does not simply speak of the physical location of your physical incarnation at a specific time and place, but of a mental and spiritual awareness. I am here speaks of your entire being coalescing around a single moment in time.

Take note of the way your clothes feel against your skin, how it feels where your body makes contact with chair or cushion or floor. Pay attention to your breathing and let your mind float freely between those things you are currently experiencing. If you notice your thoughts going to the past, or future, gently correct them back to this time and place. Be present fully in this moment and whatever it holds for you.

John Baltisberger

Loneliness

The first step is to change our syntax. Do not say "I am lonely," as the loneliness is not your identity; rather say, "I am experiencing the feeling of loneliness in this moment." This is more honest; while subjectively I can see that we are all connected, that no human is an island unto themselves, I can also be aware of the emotional weight of physical isolation. In today's world, loneliness is easier to combat on a literal level than ever. Through the use of the Internet, social media, message boards, and meet up groups, humans are able to join with others virtually no matter what their interests sway to. Often when we speak of loneliness, we mean either romantic loneliness, specific person loneliness, or event loneliness. While all of these have different goals and strategies to alleviate, the emotional resonance often feels the same.

You may spend some time identifying what sort of interaction you are missing; this will help you formulate a plan to address your needs. It is often true that as beings that are incarnated as social animals, we feed off of each other's energy. The power of interacting with like-minded peers or loved ones cannot be overstated. But it is not always possible to surround ourselves with our peers, nor is it possible to always have access to the person or persons we feel would abate our feelings of loneliness.

Therefore, we may use meditative states to look beyond the subjective need for company to finding companionship with our own dream states. I recommend against casting yourself forward into the future, in which you will be able to spend time with others, as this daydreaming detracts from your ability to be present. It may also have the side effect of deepening your subjective loneliness as you compare these future times to the one you are currently experiencing.

Instead, focus on the immediacy of the present, consider what aspects of yourself that your friends bring out that you enjoy. What are the things that your friends and loved ones make better; what are ways to nurture and grow those aspects on your own?

Though we have not covered them, reading, writing, and various art forms may all be used in meditative ways. Through the growth of those parts of you that interact with others, we may continue to evolve the self during periods of isolation.

Take several moments to center yourself; reach up towards the sky, allowing your spine to stretch. See your idealized self standing before you; this is who you wish to be, not what you wish to have or wish to achieve, but simply the person who is capable of succeeding where you wish to succeed.

Consider not what is different but what

is evolved. Through the use of self-nurturing practice and skill development, we may move ourselves closer to the self we wish to become. That self already exists in the future. All it takes to become that perfect self is to wish it and enact your willpower to evolve through practice and diligence.

Pain

The first step is to change our syntax. Do not say "I am hurting," as the pain is not your identity; rather say, "I am experiencing the feeling of pain in this moment."

One of the first visions of meditation I came in contact with was the cartoons of a yogi meditating on a bed of nails or a Buddhist monk meditating on a mountain as the elements tore at them, seemingly immune to discomfort and pain. While many people use meditating as a form of pain management, the truth is that there is nothing mystical happening here, at least nothing mystical outside the power of the self and mind over matter.

It is not magical supernatural powers that elevate these masters above sensations of pain; it is the recognition that pain is not the self, and therefore, something that may be endured. This is all to say that meditation does not destroy pain, it will not make you immune to the sensation, and frankly, you would not want it to. Though there are many—and this may include you—who suffer from chronic pain, or chronic illness which involves pain, pain remains a useful tool for the body to communicate with our conscious selves.

It is pain that lets us know an ankle is injured and that staying off of it would be wisest for its healing, it is pain that lets us know we are hungry and need to nourish ourselves, it is pain that lets us know we have been damaged in some way and we must address it. But there are also other pains, pains from old injuries, chronic pain. Pain that lets us know something isn't right, but we cannot really do anything to address it.

The first step then is to identify your pain. Do you need medical assistance? Do you need to treat a wound or eat? Whether or not you meditate at this time, if your pain is unidentified and persists, we urge you to seek medical care.

Focus on the concept of the body. We have learned that while we consider our body to be the vehicle we drive in this physical plane of existence, it is just that, a belonging and not our true selves. There is plenty of pain we sit with comfortably: tattoos, hot baths, shots, post workout muscle pain. We know we are capable of enduring pain, and so it falls on us to separate our being from the sensation. We can become capable of seeing pain as something that is experienced, but in the same way pleasure or surprise is, as a sensation that we need not dwell on in order to be whole.

Focus on your breathing, specifically the way your breath moves your body: the rise and fall of your shoulders, the way your throat and nostrils open and close to allow the breath. As you pay attention to your breath, take control of it. Much like your breath, your body is yours to control; you may allow it autonomy, but ultimately, it belongs to you.

As you focus on the area of discomfort, consider the pain as it exists; acknowledge that it is there but has no power over you other than its presence. As a warning system for your body, you may understand it has importance but has no power over you, and it is not something you need to panic or obsess over.

When you feel as though you have gained mastery over the presence of your pain, open your eyes and go about your day.

John Baltisberger

Resources

In the end, this is a book about wellness; no matter the esoteric truth or the subjective analysis of our roadblocks to peace, sometimes, what we need is help. Do not feel you have to go through any crisis alone. Do not hesitate to reach out. Below are the numbers for several national hotlines and help programs. Take care of yourself and allow yourself to be taken care of. I love you.

John Baltisberger

National Suicide Prevention Lifeline
1-800-273-8255

National Substance Use and Disorder Issues Referral and Treatment Hotline
1-800-662-HELP (4357)

Teen Life Line Phone or Text
602-248-TEEN (8336)

Veterans Crisis Line
1-800-273-8255 (**press 1**)

Addiction Hotline
1-866-294-0316

National Human Trafficking Hotline
888-373-7888

The Trevor Project (LGBTQ suicide help)
866-488-7386
(**Text**) 202-304-1200

National Domestic Violence Hotline
1-800-799-7233
Thehotline.org (**for chat**)

The Subjective Truth of the Esoteric Self

John Baltisberger

John is an enthusiast of spiritual and mental health who lives in Austin, TX. Primarily known for his horror and speculative fiction writing, John is an avid practioner of meditation, and believes that it be beneficial to anyone who seeks it. You can find more of John's work and writing at www.kaijupoet.com.

www.ingramcontent.com/pod-product-compliance
Lightning Source LLC
Chambersburg PA
CBHW071353080526
44587CB00017B/3091